<u>Dedic</u>

To Chad, Joni, Mazzy Belle and Clementine Belle

And to my heart mate, Harry

Acknowledgement

Many thanks go out to Catherine Sword and Andy Makowski for their helpful comments about this work. A warm flow of gratitude goes to Sue Reynolds for her cover art and to James Dewar for his expertise on layout and format. Thanks to both for their constant generosity around all things books, reading and writing. A special thank you from my heart rises to David Brazier of the Amida Institute for spontaneously taking the time and having the interest to offer clarifying insights about earlier stages of this book.

PREFACE

The conversation between Buddhism and neuroscience has picked up a lot of energy in the last few years. The very first meetings of the Mind and Life Institute were back in 1985, springing from the conversations between the Dalai Lama and Chilean scientist Francisco Varela. Since then, enthusiasm has grown and this dialogue has even contributed to a changing perception of science itself. Compared with thirty years ago, scientists are now much less wary of considering and investigating subjective states and evidence emerging from introspective experiments. Most recently, the sudden coming into fashion of mindfulness as a means for reducing stress, aiding healing and generally improving life quality, not just in the medical domain, but also in many areas of social life, even including business and the military, has given a further impetus to this expanding area of creative discussion. Conferences that bring together scientists and meditators are now well-attended and influential. The insights and know-how developed by ancient wisdom traditions, especially Buddhism, are now understood to provide a fund of knowledge and intriguing areas ripe for investigation by science looking for an understanding of how the brain works, what consciousness is and how it functions, how healing can be brought about for many intractable physical as well as mental conditions, and, more generally, how the mental and physical dimensions of human experience mesh.

This present short book fits into this area of discussion by drawing attention to the practices of Tibetan tantric visualisation. For centuries, tantric practitioners have been teaching methods that train the mind. Neuroscience has recently made discoveries about how training the mind is also training the brain, changing its neural pathways and even its size, shape and organisation. The brain is not the static structure that we once thought it was, but an organ that continues to grow and change throughout our lives. The way it grows and changes can be influenced by how we train our minds. These structural changes can have substantial effects upon our physical and mental wellbeing as well as upon our talents and capacities. The book focuses upon the Tibetan practice called the Medicine Buddha Empowerment as an example, but it is quite clear to the reader that the implications extend well beyond one practice or even one spiritual system.

This work, therefore, also contributes to a much-needed rapprochement between science and spirituality. If we are all to lead happier and healthier lives and maximise at least some of our latent potentials, then the results and understandings emerging from this cross-fertilisation promise to yield a very important harvest. Nor is this simply a book of theory. It is deeply rooted in the personal experience of the author and her own experience of healing. In many ways, this is a work that merely whets the appetite, for one cannot help, in reading it, wanting more.

- David Brazier

David Brazier is a Buddhist teacher. He is head of the Order of Amida Buddha, a Pureland Buddhist community, and also president of the International Zen Therapy Institute which promotes the teaching and application of Buddhist psychology. He is author of ten books on Buddhism, psychology and culture and is a published poet. He can be followed on Facebook (davidbrazierauthor), Twitter (@dharmavidya), or on the various web sites of ITZI, Amida Academy and Friends of the Amida Order. He lectures internationally with programmes in Korea, Spain and Peru as well as frequent appearances in other American, West European, and Asian countries. He holds a PhD and several professional qualifications and has authored a large number of articles, monographs and chapters in English language publications. He has a strong interest in promoting harmony between followers of different spiritual paths and in the practical application of spiritual wisdom.

Glossary

Endnotes

More

<u>MEDICINE BUDDHA/MEDICINE MIND</u>
<u>INTRODUCTION</u>

I am not a Neuroscientist. As a poet, writer and daydreamer I observe what happens when exciting connections between ideas take place. I make no claims to be a scholar or academic although I hold a double graduate degree. To top this off I am a person who struggles with faith each day, every day one step at a time toward the confidence it brings when on scant occasions faith graces my day. I was accused many times by my Meditation Teacher Namgyal Rinpoche of being a Doubting Thomas. He made it sound like the worst thing in the world. Mea Culpa.

When I stumbled upon Norman Doidge's book <u>The Brain That Changes Itself</u> some dendrites fired in my brain and I'm sure my dopamine levels heightened in response to what I saw: here in the latest science from the West lay an elegant explanation of how meditating on figures and repeating mantras, the foundation practices of Tibetan Vajrayana Tantra Buddhism, works. I gobbled the book once, then again.

What thrills me and I hope will help others is that here begins an explanation that does not demand faith. Neuroscience explains the *reason why* this form of meditation works to ease suffering, release pain and help form more positive attitudes, behaviors and life experience in those who practice diligently.

A proliferation of data from decades of research on Mindfulness Training accrues from the labs of Professor Richard Davidson at University of Wisconsin-Madison. Professor Davidson is a long time student of His Holiness the Dalai Lama, the most recognizable face for Tibetan Buddhism in the world. Davidson's data, carefully culled in part through a machine called an fMRI or functioning Magnetic Resonance Image machine, supplies Western people with a foundation of how Mindfulness meditation uplifts our brains our attitudes and our lives.

Mindfulness or Vipassana meditation is one of two main trunks in the abundant tree of meditation practices. Shamatha, which is the creation of a calm mind and body foundation through focusing on pictures, real or imagined, while reciting mantras, constitutes the other main trunk.

Encouraged by the proliferation of data about the intersection between Neuroscience and Mindfulness, I set out to discover the seam between Tibetan Buddhist Vajrayana Tantra meditation and the fascinating news arriving from Western neuroscience about how our brains work. Here then is an incomplete beginning of an exploration of Vajrayana Tantra Meditation as related to Neuroscience.

It is my hope others more skilled and accomplished than I will take up the research necessary to help the world understand the benefits of meditating on figures and reciting sounds.

In this book I refer to Vajrayana Tantra practice as any meditation that involves glancing at, gazing at, looking at, memorizing and visualizing a figure, while reciting a mantra. I recognize the path of Vajrayana Tantra, aka the Diamond Vehicle or Path, to be much more profound and enriched than this plain definition but for the purposes of this writing I must restrain the meaning.

How a new teaching grips the imaginations of people in a new land comes from many, many travelers, many teachers and nuances on a teaching as they converge. Therefore naming one particular teacher, or choosing one particular framework, as I have both with Namgyal Rinpoche and Tibetan Vajrayana Tantra, acts as an illustrative thread from which to tell the tale. In other words the practice of Tibetan Vajrayana Tantra may be substituted by many meditations in Christianity, Kabbala, Native American traditions and so on to include the panoply of world religions and spiritual practices where those include imagined visualizations and sounds. Indeed the meditations offered by Jesuits for example sculpt a fine example of what we'll learn to describe as "neurons that fire together, wire together."

While it is for certain Namgyal Rinpoche, aka Lesley George Dawson was the first recognized Vajrayana Tantra lineage holder in Canada, many enriched teachers contributed to the flourishing of Tibetan and other meditation traditions throughout the Western world.

The reference throughout this text to my personal experience with Vajrayana Tantra Buddhism is an attempt to describe the healing possible when this powerful tradition serves as a central life focus. Since my teacher Namgyal Rinpoche introduced me to most of the initiations and to the details of the practice, he figures prominently in parts of the following story. Although I continue to be grateful for his presence in my life and for the generosity with which he gave his insights, this in no way is meant to describe him as the only teacher, the only good meditation teacher, or anything like that. He is an illustrative example, as is what I offer of my personal life, to describe in human terms how the amazing mind works.

May all teachings that contribute to the elimination of suffering and the raising of wholesomeness continue to thrive.

A Personal History with VajrayanaTantra Meditation

The man sitting inside the grey concrete room wore different clothes and head accessories this day than he had the four previous days I'd attended. A colorful headband rose across his forehead into five points, the central point at the center of his forehead. Turquoise ribbons braided within his long brown hair cascaded down either shoulder. His bright yellow vest marked with burgundy, purple, green designs overlay his torso leaving his brown arms bare. Burgundy robes splayed around him from the waist down, like a dark wine fountain flowing around where he sat on the first tier of the simple dais.

Above him by a couple of feet, sat another Tibetan man, His Holiness Chogyam Rinpoche, Master Key Holder in all sects of Tibetan Buddhism and our transmission teacher. This man, his round bald head bare, his robes simple in contrast with the ceremonial regalia of the man with the turquoise earrings His Holiness Sakya Trizen,[1] this Chogyam Rinpoche burbled along fluently in Tibetan and His Holiness the Sakyapa, twenty-seven years

---

[1] His Holiness Sakya Trizen heads the sect of Tibetan Buddhism called Sakya. For more on the other sects and their heads see Endnotes.

old, quickly translated sometimes for hours on end, into easily understood English.

Standing at attention surrounding these two, several monks varying by age but uniform in burgundy robes stood passively until they suddenly leapt about the room, gracefully pouring rice into our cupped hands, spraying water sprinkles from the ends of a peacock feather, flashing pictorial cards in front of our eyes so quickly I was not able to see the forms and shapes, only a mere blur of color. It was just more movement in this kaleidoscope of Tibetan ritual.

We sat day after day, some days long into the evening, receiving the blessings, chanting the verses, our hands at our chests in prayer mudra or cupped to receive the rice, or resting on our knees where we sat.

I often gazed at the small windows high in the walls letting in the light of day. I watched that light turn to slanted rays of orange flames of dusk. The room had been built with the extreme harshness of Tibetan winters in mind but here in Dehra Dun, India the problem might more easily be tuberculosis among the monks, brought on by the mild climate and heavier air.

It was November of 1972 and over one hundred of us had gathered, many at the behest of our root Teacher, Namgyal Rinpoche, from various parts of the planet to receive what His Holiness Chogyam Rinpoche and His Holiness the Sakyapa, out of their respect for our Teacher, so generously offered to bestow: the precious Wongs.

I knew nothing about any of this. Instead I sat on the cold hard concrete floor aware my ability to fold into a full lotus posture garnered me cachet, as though this gift of genetic height and flexibility also implied more mature spiritual understanding. The rice seeds crunched in my mouth, dry and unsatisfying but supplying a tiny distraction from the on going sounds of Tibetan words, flowing peacock feathers, the annoying presence of some good looking monks whose eyes did not return my gaze.

Some of my family had preceded me on this adventure. I had come because of a vision that arose in my apartment in Toronto; I had come because even if I didn't like this Namgyal Rinpoche, he was the most interesting person in my small purview; I had come because even I knew my home city held all the joys that continued to waste my days and nights: bars, music, drugs and men. I was there because I did not know where else to be, what else to do with this life. I was there because my feelings about life were simple: I didn't want it. Occasionally a tiny spiritual aspiration flickered off and on, a minute candle in the midnight storms of my unrepentant, undisciplined and self-indulgent psyche. In short I was desperate.

I recall I walked the dusty road outside the monastery walls during twilight, watching the orange light from the setting sun flare and then soften to deep purples, blues. I sang as I walked that road past the dingy houses, sad stray dogs whose eyes held unremitting sorrow, past the trees whose branches seemed heavy with the weight of the dung smoke laden air. I sang Bob Dylan's recently released album "Nashville Skyline"; Crosby, Stills, Nash and Young's album "Déjà vu"; Simon and Garfunkle's album "Scarboro Fair." I knew the words to every song on each of these albums and more. I sang out loud longing for a bar, for drugs, for booze, for a way back home. I sang and watched those longings rise, tear inside my chest and throw me into tears of misery and grief. I kept singing.

In the hotel where my relatives had settled near the monastery, I had slung my sleeping bag over the bed of ropes, large ropes strung across a solid wooden frame. I vowed, once back where western beds were available I would never again leave their comfort.

Those days in Dehra Dun we understood very little or nothing about what was going on in the time we spent inside the Sakya Temple. We accepted consciously or unconsciously that being in that room, sitting passively while rice fell on our heads, shoulders, the floor all round, accepting the sprinkles of water streaming from the peacock's bright tail feather which shook in our direction from the Monk's hand, the intonations in a foreign language, we accepted that somehow all of this had some power to help us in our meditation practice and our lives.

Finally one or two among us approached His Holiness Sakya Trizen with a request for some teaching on the ceremonies and some answers to our question, "What is this all about?"

The first day after His Holiness agreed to give teaching on Wongs, I held pages of white paper still smelling of ink from the copying machine that had created them. The outlines and instructions of Wong appeared incompletely on those pages but with the diligence of keen kindergarten children some of us believed repetition would lead to more understanding.

I had no idea then that those pages, and the many hours of, days of meditation practice to follow, held the power to nurture mental health and a feeling of well being out of the chaos and damage of my ravaged psyche.

Wongs: The Central Ceremony of Tibetan Buddhist Vajrayana Tantra

Before we begin to navigate the exciting world of basic Neuroscience and start the dance of parallel viewing between Tibetan Vajrayana Tantra and Neuroscience, we must take in a little information. The central ceremony in Tibetan Vajrayana Tantra is called a Wong*[2]. It is also known as an Empowerment.

Each deity or personified figure has his or her own Wong. Wongs ceremonially encase all the teachings of Tibetan Vajrayana Tantra, introduce the meditation practitioner to the shapes, size, color and in some cases activities of the central character of that specific Wong. Hidden in the Wongs lie geometry in the symmetry of the human form, the history of the Tibetan culture and deep

---

[2] For more on Wongs or Empowerments go to www.khandro.net click on site map and scroll down on the left hand side to Tibetan Buddhism. Click and again scroll down on the left hand side to find the word Empowerment. Click on that for a clear, simple but full explanation of the role these ceremonies play in Vajrayana Tantra.

instructions on how to practice this meditation for one who understands how to read the symbols.

For our purposes simply understand that Wongs include instructions about the meditation practice for the Wong's central character, sometimes called a Deity. For example during the Wong of the Medicine Buddha students hear and see the complete visualization of Medicine Buddha unfolding in exactly the order to be repeated when the student practices at home.

The Wong is the template. The on going practice is what helps mind/heart unfold.

Vajrayana Tantra meditation differs from the now ubiquitous Mindfulness in form. Both carry the practitioner to the same increased mental and emotional health as documented by Professor Richard Davidson, but with a difference. As stated above Mindfulness requires paying attention to the breath as it flows in and out of the body and to the body as the breath flows in and out. Vajrayana Tantra on the other hand engages the meditating mind with a picture of the figure and a mantra, or prayer, to be recited aloud.

Some notes by His Holiness the 17th Gyalwang Karmapa, head of the Karma Kagyu sect of Tibetan Buddhism, may help clarify the differences between Vajrayana Tantra and Vipassana. In April of 2015 His Holiness the Karmapa made a visit to Mount Laurel New Jersey, USA. From notes from that day we learn, "Presenting meditation within a Buddhist context, His Holiness (the 17th Gyalwang Karmapa) explained that in general there are two types—placement meditation and analytical meditation. Without the foundation of shamatha, which is considered placement meditation, it would be very difficult to develop vipassana." [3]

Therefore we can take with confidence the understanding of His Holiness the Karmapa that meditation practice resolves into one of two types: shamatha, meaning the development of calm and vipassana meaning the development of insight. Shamatha practices envelope or contain the Wongs. There is more but for our purposes we will leave the descriptions there.

---

[3] Mount Laurel Karmapa Visit...During First Dharma Center Visit, Karmapa teaches on...(April 4, 2015 Mount Laurel New Jersey)

Namgyal Rinpoche said meditating with vipassana is like having an operation without anesthetic, while shamatha is the same operation with anesthetic.

Tibetan VajrayanaTantra depends for its essence on these ceremonies, the Wongs. It is understood among Tibetans that without receiving the Wong it is of some benefit to practice meditation. However, with the proper Wong given from a qualified transmission Teacher, the meditator's practice deepens, enlivens and yields fruit.

A useful metaphor may be to consider the transmission experience, or Wong as the fuel that makes the vehicle's engine turn over, thus enabling the drive.

A specific Wong ceremony reveals for participants how a figure emerges from a point called Sunyata. In the early Twentieth Century when Buddhism first crossed out of Tibet via books, the word Sunyata was poorly translated to mean "nothing" or "nothingness," evoking a misconception that Buddhism had to do with Nihilism. Nihilism, a concept developed by Western philosophy, was enjoying a moment of fame in the early Twentieth Century thus its reference to Buddhism at that time made sense, however erroneous.

Sunyata more properly matches what quantum physicists refer to as the "soup" or essence of nothing from which everything spontaneously arises. Western physicists trace the paths of positrons rising from this "soup" and have determined these pathways indicate where form will rise.

In Wongs the meditator tries to imagine this same "soup" or emptiness from which anything may rise at any moment in any direction. During the Wong most instructions include the idea that out of Sunyata arises a flower.

The meditator visualizes a flower with many petals in full bloom. This may not happen the first, second or tenth time a person tries but eventually the human ability to create visualized forms and colors flows more easily. Out of this flower the main figure typically rises spontaneously (oh, that soup!) sitting or standing on it with as many arms and legs as the originators may have experienced. One starts with imagination of these pictorial images and, as we shall see, from repetitive imagination emerges the skill to visual.

Along with this visualization the Teacher offers a mantra by reciting perhaps as many as three times out loud the sound associated with the figure.

In the early days, we approached Namgyal, "What is the correct way to pronounce these mantras, Sir?"

"It is impossible," he explained, "to recite the same mantra once, " and left it at that. So we learned to do our best and as instructed, leave it at that.

Namgyal Rinpoche in his enthusiasm and generosity concerning all activities that may release people from suffering and lead to an ultimate freedom, offered to transmit three Wongs for those interested to attend. It was 1971. Thus a small group of students made their way to the Dharma Center of Canada to receive what was being described as a "precious opportunity": the transmission of Vajrayana Tantra. As it turned out, the first experience at the Dharma Center was taking Refuge, not a Wong proper. However in months to follow on different places around the planet Namgyal Rinpoche bestowed many Wongs upon hundreds of students.

Where did this path of ceremonially encased ritual begin? Who first brewed the stew of Wongs? Although we may never know the exact person, the legendary Padmasambhava often takes credit for being the first cook of ritual Wongs.

A Brief History of Vajrayana Tantra
A Trace of Mysticism

The legendary Shaman and Teacher Padmasambhava traveled out of his native India sometime in the 8th century ACE to the wild northern lands known as Tibet. There he encountered a kind of mysticism based on what we might think of today as Voo-Doo: the power of casting spells, the powers of magic. This mysticism was called Bon.

Because the Bon tradition with its ritual incantations and spell making already existed, Padmasambhava, eager to convert these Tibetans to the new way of living called Buddhism, took major aspects of the Bon ceremonies and wove those with his profound insight into the teachings of the Buddha who had lived in India over a hundred centuries prior.

The insight of Padmasambhava, that cultures are most easily persuaded toward a new religion through similarities to the old one, echoes our knowledge of the Pre-Christ roots of Christianity. In Zoroastrianism a star above a humble shed, some members of the elite journeying toward a new infant, shepherds on watch noticing fantastic events unfolding in the night sky, all blend into our story of Christ's birth.

Padmasambhava's legendary mysticism fell upon my ears this way. A Teacher may speak about the history of the Wong. The history opens a peek into the mythological or perhaps real history of that initiation ceremony, that specific Wong. Namgyal Rinpoche before entering with us into the Wong of Padmasambhava, revealed some of the stories surrounding this legendary figure.

Padmasambhava traveled through Tibet and came across a tavern, rolls one such story. Being thirsty he entered the humble building. We imagine the native Tibetans seeing this man from India with his strange clothes, peculiar hair and odd habits. We may imagine suspicion and a restless sense of danger rising among the customers and bartender.

Padmasambhava asks for a drink. The bartender, taking note of the change in the air, the tension in the faces around him, says, "Nothing here for you."

Padmasambhava repeats his request. The bartender again refuses. A third time.

Finally Padmasambhava slides from its sheath his purba, (a ceremonial curved knife reputed to destroy demons) slams it into the wooden bar, crying, "Then the sun will not set until you do!"

Customers mumble among themselves, some mocking, sneering at this upstart with his outrageous claims. The more superstitious glance with growing anxiety toward the oddly dressed stranger and beyond him, the sun.

As the first day passes into night, then the second, and the sun stays in the same spot, others from the countryside having heard through the grapevine of these happenings begin to filter into the tiny tavern. Some beg the bartender to reconsider. Their flocks, herds and domestic animals, their wives are upset and complaining and they themselves feel the dread upon the land of this supernatural experience.

Finally on the third day the bartender pours the drink, imploring Padmasambhava, "Let the sun set! Only let the sun set!" He puts the drink in front of the great Mystic and the sun does what the sun is supposed to do.

When I first heard it I enjoyed this story for its mythological size and content. I did not believe it. Namgyal Rinpoche bestowed the Guru Rinpoche Empowerment (the Padmasambhava Wong) more than once, each time revealing another aspect of Padmasambhava's miraculous powers and his predictions.

Padmasambhava left a legacy of predictions, one of the most famous being, "When the Iron Horse runs on tracks and the Silver Bird flies, the Tibetan people will be scattered across the Earth like ants." This translates easily into the understanding that when trains run along the ground and airplanes fly the Tibetan diaspora will begin. Check.

Padmasambhava went on to describe some of the events to come in what is known as the "Kali Yuga" or our current times. Kali refers to the Hindi Goddess of Time, Change and Destruction. A Yuga is an unimaginably long period of time. Padmasambhave predicted mass insanity with mass murders taking place for no reason.

Certainly prior to our times and likely during the times of Padmasambhava mass executions delivered with a sense of revenge, perhaps even a feeling of justice by many who felt insulted, disobeyed, ripped off, in short poorly treated, took place.

What this Mystic's predication stated was that the increase in numbers of mass killings would spring from no political turmoil, no religious fervor, no immediate cause save the insanity of the killer. Padmasambhava said mental illness would get bad enough that people in large cities would step over the dead bodies lying in the street, so immune would they be to death.

This happened during the Communist uprising in the '30's and '40's. My Russian mother-in-law remembered having to walk around a decomposing corpse lying on the street in her village after the Communists came and shot the person, presumably to send a message. The message was received: if you showed any response to the corpse, you too would be shot.

Padmasambhava's predictions outline a time when some, crying for help on the streets, would be greeted with blank stares and empty gazes from those passing by. Street people? The homeless?

In the decades since I first heard of him and his predictions, I have always found a strange sense of comfort in knowing some of the worst of our times, tragedies like the Columbine shooting and on, had been foreseen by Padmasambhava. The comfort races before the thought: if he knew, couldn't he prevent it?

How Vajrayana Tantra Came to Toronto

I met my teacher when he was called Bikkhu Ananda Bodhi, meaning Blissful Wanderer. This was in the late 1960's when all things magical and Transcendental from mind expansion to something called complete freedom rose as promises from every song, poem, every favored social event. The constraints of a conservative culture from the '50's washed away in the romantic determinism of a generation determined to end a war (they succeeded), determined to gain mental freedom, determined to learn to love. It was a very tall order although we, in the cultural naivety of a generation both young and protected, believed it all to be both imminent and not terribly difficult.

Meeting this Teacher fulfilled every poetic suggestion the magical '60's offered. Here was a Magic Man, a Healer, a Teacher of Great and Other Worldly matters. Here was a man who addressed the questions that tore at my soul: why bother living, what is the point of life, why make effort?

He responded to these questions although I never actually posed them. He just spoke. And when he spoke different and mystical events transpired. He encouraged question and exploration. He created a world in which hope and adventure galloped across a planet brimming with possibility, now! Now! Now!

He himself had been born in the East End of Toronto in the now glamorous Beach area, then a working class refuge. Raised by a Presbyterian Scots mother, a nurse, and an Irish Cop who fulfilled all the stereotypes, young Lesley George Dawson was a child extraordinary. His intelligence put him into a rigorous five year high school curriculum at 12 years of age and on to graduation when he was just 15.

In his late teens a brief stint in politics led to an invitation to speak at the Russian Presidium, which he did before heading back to England where he found himself living at the Salvation Army for lack of funds. There he heard about a Burmese Monk, one Sayadaw U Thila Wunta who was to speak at a local gathering.

This young Dawson, a prodigy in his own right, was so impressed by what the Sayadaw had to say he ventured up after the talk.

"I want to know what you know," he recounted to us years later.

The Sayadaw instructed Dawson to meet up with him in India. So with no means but a heart full of faith, Dawson set out for India.

When he arrived at the place and time agreed upon, he was told the Sayadaw was in Burma! With unremitting determination Dawson continued, finally finding this renowned healer in his native Burma. There, Dawson completed every exercise, every aspect of meditation in short order. By some accounts he completed his training in five years, by some accounts ten. In any case his genius flourished in regard to mediation as it had in academics and he achieved in less than a decade what many people aspire to attain over several lifetimes.

Dawson returned to Canada via England, landing back finally in Canada in the early 1960's. He was by then a Burmese initiate by the name of Bikkhu Ananda Bodhi, or Blissful Wanderer. He sponsored one Trungpa Rinpoche to come to the west. Trungpa of course traveled to Colorado in the US where many Tibetans, having previously trained with the CIA, lived. Here Trungpa established the Naropa Institute.

I met Namgyal Rinpoche in 1969 because someone dragged me away from drugs and partying long enough to attend a class. I was seventeen. Contrary to present day sentimentality about meeting one's Teacher, loving him or her instantly, I didn't even like him much, a feeling he returned and which lay between us for the next thirty of the thirty five years I knew, traveled and studied with him. He was contentious to say the least. He would likely have said the same about me.

It came to my ears in 1970 we, his students, were to receive the first Empowerment, of three he declared necessary for us to attain Complete Awakening. He believed sincerely we, like he himself, might achieve this coveted state easily and quickly, within at most, the next decade.

In our innocence we believed three was the total number of Empowerments or Wongs, to be had. We believed that participating in these three ceremonies, receiving the Teacher's blessings in this way meant total Enlightenment, full ease of living, full expanse of consciousness, a life without suffering, in other words full mimicry of the Bikkhu, was only a few days, a few mantras, a bit of meditation away. We had no idea.

What he bestowed that fall of 1970 was Refuge. He gave each attendee a full private audience in the comfort of Tara Cabin on the land the Dharma Centre of Canada, bought for him by his students,. Although the Refuge he bestowed was ceremonial, complete with clipping bits of hair from the top of our heads and dropping three spots of candle wax on that place, this was not a Wong.

In 1971 the Bikkhu Ananda Bodhi completed a pilgrimage to India, venturing to Rumtek Monastery where His Holiness the Sixteenth Gyalwang Karmapa, head of the Karma Kagyu sect of Tibetan Buddhism, declared this tall, thin Caucasian to be the lineage Teacher known as the Namgyal or Bearer of the Victorious Banner of the Teaching to the New World. Dawson's new full moniker became Karma Tenzin Dorje Namgyal Rinpoche.

The recognition of this young upstart from Canada, a white man, caused no end of trouble among the Tibetans who have institutionalized a belief that only men, only Tibetan men, and only Tibetan men of suitable rank or financial prowess may be recognized as Enlightened. The culture of Tibet must not be confused with the benefits of their mind science, the meditations.

Also it is very clear Namgyal Rinpoche although honored by His Holiness the 16th Gyalwang Karmapa in this way was not the only teacher to bring the ancient Tibetan Vajrayana Tantra to the rest of the world. He was however my teacher.

Namgyal Rinpoche traveled India and everywhere he went people showered him with arcane stacks of important documents (the teachings from various Wongs and meditations) ceremonial hats, robes, vases, dorjes, bells, in short all the holy paraphernalia important for the rituals of Wongs.

Thus Namgyal Rinpoche returned to Canada fully equipped to bestow Wongs, and to teach the power of visualization and mantra practice meditation known as Tantra.

Over the years Namgyal Rinpoche bestowed at least once, but often many times, all the forty major vibrations or figures of Tibetan Vajrayana Buddhism to a vast array of students around the globe. He established retreat centers in many parts of the world. In this way he fulfilled His Holiness the 16th Gyalwang Karmapa's vision of the young Western man. Namgyal Rinpoche confounded the traditions of Tibetan culture, and helped spread, like Johnny Apple Seed, the powerful technique of healing and mind expansion known as Vajrayana Tantra.

Having explored a little of the history of Vajrayana Tantra, and some of its arrival in Canada, we turn now to an elementary understanding of neuroscience.

An Elementary Understanding of Neuroscience

To navigate the exciting, perplexing world of

neuroscience, we need a simple understanding of neurons,

the cells that comprise our brains. According to Rita Carter, author of <u>Mapping the Mind,</u> neurons are, "The cells that actually create brain activity…cells which are adapted to carry an electrical signal from one to another…Each neuron connects with up to ten thousand neighbors."[4]

Comprised of billions of neurons, or brains cells, our brains light up with tiny electrical charges when the neurons connect. For example, neurons connect when we perform an action. As we perform the same action repetitively the circuits of those connecting neurons grow larger. As those circuits grow larger, it becomes increasingly natural, and increasingly easy, to repeat the action associated. These circuits may be measured on fMRI machines, functional Magnetic Resonance Imaging Machines. The results are called scans. Using such scans scientists have turned all previous knowledge about our brains and how they work upside down.

As the neurons change, the physical shape of our brain changes. This capacity of the brain to change its

---

[4] Rita Carter, <u>Mapping the Mind,</u> (London, England The Orion Group, 1988), 14

shape in response to actions and as we will see even to imaginary exercises, indeed, to the smallest of our thoughts is called "plasticity." Not only can the brain change, the brain changes constantly and continues to morph in response to our actions, speech or thoughts, whatever our attention focuses upon.

Neurons are the brain's cells, running in lengths of anywhere from very, very short to extremely long, up to six feet or more. Neurons connect to each other and form axons, the longest electrical charge carrying cables in our bodies. Springing off neurons, tiny formations that look very much like tree branches in November in Eastern Canada, barren and not touching but reaching toward each other, form. These are called dendrites. Dendrites reach toward each other but do not touch. Instead they connect via a tiny electrical charge.

Surrounding the gap between dendrites is a cell containing neurotransmitters. As the word implies, neurotransmitters facilitate the tiny electrical charge that leaps from one dendrite to another. Neurotransmitters have names like norepinephrine, acetylcholine, oxytocin and dopamine. Dopamine is our most commonly known neurotransmitter; it carries the feel good sensation you have after physical exercise.

Each of the neurotransmitters has a specific use. For example, oxytocin flushes the lush feeling lactating mothers experience with their baby at their breast. This feeling leads to a desire for more intimacy with the desired object, in this case the nursing baby. Those feelings describe the intense bond between mother and baby, nature's way of ensuring the little one's survival.

Whenever we speak, act or even think, untold numbers of dendrites light up, stoking an electrical charge that runs along a neuron and since neurons like to chat with their neighbors, other neurons join in. These others are especially encouraged to join whenever the same action, the same speech, the same thought occurs.

For instance, as I type this page, my neuronal circuits light up in approximately the same way they did yesterday when I typed. It is fractionally easier for me today than yesterday and we can know my neuronal pathways are slightly larger.

The phrase for this in neural science is "Neurons that fire together, wire together." That simple phrase will guide us as we journey through the intriguing but esoteric world of neuroscience.

The incremental ease with which you do something, say learn a new musical instrument, flows from the physiological change in your brain's structure. Plasticity means your physical actions, your emotional states, even the most fleeting of thoughts change the physical structure of your brain. With that change in physiology your brain may change your mind.

Likewise, when input arrives through our sense doors to our brains, that input changes every second of every day the structure of our brains. Brain plasticity works from outside information arriving at our perceptual base as well as from what we perceive as internal stimuli, our thoughts, feelings and sensations.

We will explore the reciprocity of flow between the outer senses and the inner states of thought, feelings and sensations as exemplified in Tibetan Tantric meditations. These meditations describe how any visualized meditations help change our minds. For now we continue our short and incomplete history of Neuroscience.

An Incomplete History of Neuroscience

Within a few years of Lesley George Dawson's birth
in the 1930's neurosurgeon Wilder Penfield made history
at the Montreal Neurological Institute by mapping
patient's brains. To Penfield, mapping meant
"…finding where in the brain different parts of the body
were represented and their activities processed."[5]

Since there are no pain receptors in the brain,
Penfield's patients remained conscious while he mapped
sensory and motor parts of the brain. He did this as he
performed surgery for brain cancer or epilepsy and an

---

[5] Norman Doidge, The Brain That Changes Itself, (New
York, Penguin Group, 2007), 48

invaluable trove of information rose out of Penfield's work for future neuroscientists.

In spite of Penfield's extraordinary attempts, Western scientists including neuroscientists continued to believe the brain developed until about the age of 14 years and then stopped. The accepted truth was that no further changes were possible. If stroke for example happened, the patient had to make do with whatever brain function was left. This view held sway in all proper scientific communities for over one hundred years.

Yet on the other side of the world meditation teachers encouraged students to practice repeating the visualization process and the repetition of mantras. The practice consisted of little more than that. Simply repeat, repeat and then repeat again.

No two sides of insight and understanding might have been further apart, the West with empirical science living in certainty that the brain, and therefore the mind including behaviors, affects, and identity, could not be changed and the simple assurances of Tibetan meditation Masters to just keep repeating the process and change, significant change, would occur.

What was about to happen in the West would set the science community on fire and stand everything known about the brain literally on its head.

Research as far back as the 1960's conducted by one Joseph Altman provided the scientific community of the day with chuckles, as they scratched their heads in amusement that this young man believed, from his research on rodents, the human brain capable of neurogenesis or growing new cells. Everyone knew with the certainty of flat earth such a thing was blatantly untrue.

Along came Elizabeth Gould in the late 1980's who researched the "…lethal effects of stress and impoverished environments on neurons, particularly the hippocampus (a limbic organ intimately associated with memory)"[6]. When she discovered the number of neurons outstripping her expectations Ms. Gould walked into the Rockefeller Institute's records on research into neurology and found the paper by Altman. His paper supported her findings.

At the same time through a belief that eerily twinned the complete conviction of Tibetan Meditation Masters'

---

[6] Stephen Larsen, Ph.D., The Neuro-feedback Solution, (Vermont, Healing Arts Press, 2012), 28

knowledge that repetition changes the brain, one Dr. Taub began treating stroke victims by reversing the usual order of things. He believed in neuroplasticity, the ability of our brains to reform, physiologically, to change their shape especially in response to physical experience. Taub believed our brains change their shape and therefore their *function* in response to physical motion and that with the right kind of training even after stroke, the brain had the ability to heal.

Until Taub's contentious experiments on monkeys at his Silver Springs Laboratory, every doctor knew if a patient lost the use of her left side to stroke, for instance, she had to adapt by stretching the power of her still healthy right side. The healthy right side was seen as the compensatory tool for the now and forever useless left side.

Eventually the maverick Taub opened a revolutionary clinic for stroke victims. Stroke sufferers, willing to try anything to recover, had their good arm taped down forcing use of the non-responsive stroke affected side, in a process he called Constraint-Induced Therapy.

After many repetitions of action the brains of these people developed new neuronal pathways that carried the signals of the affected limbs, in some cases as well as the pre-stroke condition. This meant the person who previously would have been consigned to a one-sided life, a life with only one half of their body working, now might with effort expect some return to what pre-stroke life looked like.

The effort required amounted to repeating the desired physical movement much in the same way we sat, repeating mantras and building the same visualization over and over again when we practiced Vajrayana Tantra meditations. The difference was Taub's patients exercised physically.

Taub's medical breakthroughs helped herald a new era in Western medical science. His innovative approach to stroke treatments, Constraint-Induced Therapy, helped scientists learn what really happens with neural pathways, thereby reframing all our knowledge about the brain.

Building on the work of scientists who had come before them, neuroscientists such as Michael Merzenich began to be able, "…to decode the communication of neurons, brain cells, of which the adult human brain has approximately 100 billion."[7]

Michael Merzenich, an icon in neuroscience communities provided numerous discoveries about our brains. Just one of his discoveries took the work of Penfield to the next level. Merzenich revealed these maps drawn so painstakingly by Penfield and others "…are neither immutable within a single brain cell nor universal but vary in their borders and size from person to person…the shape of our brain maps changes depending upon what we do over the course of our lives."[8]

Let's take a step back. What neuroscience determined is that our brains have a map of our bodies, an entire map detailing where in space our bodies and each body part exist right now. These maps are as unique as our fingerprints, or our taste buds. Truly we are in every way individuals. We are individuals who can and do change in response to the actions, behavior, speech and thought we offer to our world and that we take in from our world.

---

[7] Doidge, op. cit., p. 48.
[8] Ibid., p. 49.

Another giant in the history of neuroscience is V.S. Ramachandran. A tall man whose love of language matches his fire for science, Ramachandran opened the gates to relieving pain through the application of simple, elegant experiments in neuroplasticity.

Building on Taub's understandings, Ramachandran has helped thousands of people who suffered from phantom pain. In doing so he set the stage for an increased understanding of how our brains map our bodies.

Indulging in his life long interest in phantom limbs and the pain that so often accompanies such phantom limbs, and disenchanted with elaborate technologies, Ramachandran designed a cake box and mirror tool, based on his assumption he could fool the brain of patients afflicted with phantom pain injury.

He took a large cake box sized box without a top. He placed a divider down the middle so two sections sit side by side. Each has a hole in the front of the box, a hole large enough for a man's fist and arm to slide through. The divider down the middle of the box holds a mirror on one side.

Ramachandran asked an amputee who suffered from excruciating elbow pain from his amputated left arm, to place his good right arm into the right side of the box where the mirror was. Then the man imagined placing his amputated left arm into the hole on the right side of the box. The mirror picked up the image of his right arm as though it was the amputated left arm. This exercise of the imagined left arm entering the box allowed the patient's brain, which had maintained a pre-amputation map of the body including the left arm, to respond as though the left arm was intact.

To the delight and joy of the sufferer once his eyes identified in the mirror a physical image of his otherwise invisible left arm and once he moved his physically present right arm, which sent the brain into believing the non-existent left arm had moved, the phantom movement relieved much of his pain.

However it was soon evident in order to experience relief the man had to sit with his eyes glued to the mirror. In other words his brain had rewired the circuitry of the phantom limb to a small degree, but whenever he withdrew his hands and his eyes left the mirror, his brain reverted to its old highways.

This is what happens. We start in something new with a narrow neuronal pathway through our brains. This is the initial stage of a new action or experience. As the action or experience repeats, that narrow pathway grows wider and deeper because "Neurons that fire together, wire together." The more you do or think or feel something, the easier it is to do, think or feel the same thing.

Ramachandran then gave the mirror box to his patient to take home and use for ten minutes a day. In four weeks his patient called, joyously exclaiming not only was the former pain in his phantom limb completely gone, but the phantom limb itself, a limb the patient had been feeling hanging uselessly at his side for ten years, was gone too!

Through neuroplasticity and a simple tool, Ramachandran had devised a way to help the brain rewire itself away from the old pattern that had included the phantom limb. In the words of Norman Doidge, "V.S. Ramachandran the neurological illusionist, had become the first physician to perform a seemingly impossible operation: the successful amputation of a phantom limb."[9]

The ability of our brains to rewire out of a pattern that signals pain into a new pattern exclusive of pain had been established. The Tantric technique of gazing at Medicine Buddha repeatedly while citing mantras focusing on the serenity and calm health of this extra-human representation encourages just such a shift in the brains of meditators.

Medicine Buddha Visualization

Medicine Buddha practice is one of the few Wongs and meditation practices traditionally given out to the public. Many Tibetan Empowerments or Wongs require permission from the Teacher. That Teacher may easily

---

[9] Ibid, p. 187.

demand a large number of other meditations, called the Ngon Drol or Foundation Practices, be completed first.

Because Medicine Buddha was traditionally available to all and because the figure itself is of one head, two arms, two legs, following the expected human design and not, like many Tibetan iconographical depictions, multi-headed, many armed and legged, I chose it for the purpose of this book.

I offer a few words in general about meditation. First, your mind will wander. That's its nature. Any teacher, program or exercise that claims you'll reach a state where your mind stops wandering ought be avoided. Do not be dismayed then but gently return your wandering mind, as you would a beloved child, back to the object of your focus.

What you are training is not the wandering mind but the part of your mind that knows how to focus. When that focusing part gets stronger, you will notice it more than the wandering mind. Therefore you will no longer be concerned about whether your mind wanders or not because you will feel confident in your ability to focus appropriately when needed.

So the first exercise in all meditation is to bring your wandering mind back over and over. That requires that you notice the wandering. That's all you need do. Notice and return. Notice and return.

The idea of sitting in full lotus posture supports the practices of yogis who retire from the world to devote their whole lives to their practice. It also works well, if the meditator can do it without undo pain, while in full retreat. For a daily or even weekly practice, find a straight chair, place feet on the floor, uncrossed at the ankle and maintain a relatively straight spine. That last is the most important point.

Begin every meditation session with a few deep breaths down as far into the diaphragm as possible.

Now for our chosen meditation focus: Medicine Buddha. He sits serenely upon a fully opened flower. You may imagine a lotus or carnation, or water lily to get the sense of it. His body and face are a deep blue in color, the color of Lapis Lazuli. Namgyal Rinpoche encouraged us to visualize this blue shot through with veins of gold.

His left hand holds in his lap a bowl filled with the complete nectar of healing and immortality. His right arm extends easefully across his right knee where his right thumb and index finger hold the stem of a flower or herb, called the Myrobalan flower, said to be the antidote for every sickness throughout time. In Western Alchemy this was called the Panacea, an object of much devoted search.

He is the embodiment of serenity and stability. He wears the robes of an ordinary monk, patched and orange and yellow in color.

That's it. His mantra is "Tadyata Om Bekandze, Bekandze, Maha Bekandze Radza Samugate Soha."

Tibetan culture holds a belief that syllables of language contain sacred power and when sounded those syllables create energetic vibratory pathways. Those pathways when focused upon strongly enough and when vibrated correctly may, they believe, change physical form itself.

When we translate the syllables, which in Tibetan sound rich, mellifluous and satisfying, we are left with the English, "May the many sentient beings who are sick quickly be freed from sickness and may all the sicknesses of beings never arise again."

Many recordings of this deep and sonorously intoned mantra are easily available on the Internet. I encourage you to find one that feels good to you. Listen to it often, sensing as you do so what happens in your body.

The Neuroscience of Brain Maps

It's important to learn a little about Brain Maps. Each of us, as Merznich et al discovered, has in the wiring of our neural pathways a map of our bodies.

Most of us easily accept the notion that our brains hold a map of our bodies. Most of us intuitively feel this map is stable, unchanging, providing us with the same boundary information no matter what the circumstances we experience. However, read what we learn from Norman Doidge in a simple experiment with V.S.Ramachandran about the body and body maps.

"(Ramachandran) told me to put my right hand under the table, so my hand was hidden. Then he tapped the tabletop with one hand, while with his other he tapped mine under the table where I couldn't see it, in an identical rhythm. When he moved the spot where he hit the tabletop, a bit to the left or the right, he moved his hand under the table exactly the same way. After a few minutes I stopped experiencing him as tapping my hand under the table and instead—fantastic as it sounds—started to feel that the body image of hand had merged with the tabletop so that the sensation of being tapped seemed to come from the tabletop. He had created an illusion in which my sensory body image had now been expanded to include a piece of furniture!"[10]

Doidge found the boundary of his hand removed and a new boundary, a new sense of belonging as it were, with the top of a table! This extraordinary, simple exercise demonstrates clearly the brain map we have of our bodies and our boundaries is not rigid but flows and shifts with only a few minutes of experience in our world. It is as if we are all shape shifters or chameleons, prepared to accept new boundaries according to our environment.

This notion helps us understand how meditating on Medicine Buddha helps erase some of our usually felt sense of who we are, and replaces it with an identity that includes the serenity, peacefulness and wisdom of Medicine Buddha.

A subtle incongruence fills the last couple of pages about body maps. If neurons that fire together wire

---

[10] Doidge op. cit., p.189-190.

together, what happens in our body maps regarding the difference between those parts we use a lot, like our mouths, hands, or feet, and those parts we use less frequently? The answer is the difference does register and gives rise to a very peculiar human shape, one in which the hands and feet, the mouth and lips are disproportionately large compared to the arms, legs, or behind. You may find this image easily by typing in Cortical Homunculus and scrolling down. You'll see the image of what we look like if we saw the proportion of neurons used: extremely large lips, hands, and feet for instance.

It's Just Imagination

Since my introduction to Tibetan Tantric meditation in that building in India all those years ago, I have continued with the meditation practices struggling mightily at some points and sailing effortlessly at others, for over forty years. What drew me back to this form of meditation was the experience, after every meditation session, of feeling just a little bit better. Did I imagine this or was some change actually happening?

I experienced a healing through the power of Tantric meditation. But I did not know how it had taken place, how simply by repeating certain sounds or glancing at a painted figure depicting love or compassion, or even wrath, I had grown so beyond depression, addictions and despair to a full life where the undercurrent is one of peaceful wellbeing. How did meditation help effect what was to me a miraculous transformation? Was it just my imagination that meditation had helped?

As a meditation teacher of some thirty years I have encountered the same question coming from the mouths of many people interested in meditation, "Isn't it all just in your imagination?"

Now thanks to neuroscience we know the answer is yes. Further we now know from the results in explorations in neuroscience, imagination is all we need to provide the positive changes in brain structure and function we seek. Here's how.

An Australian scientist, G.L. Moseley found that many of his phantom limb patients did not have success using just the Mirror Box developed by V.S. Ramachandran. Many of Moseley's phantom limb patients had such severe pain from their phantom limbs they could not move their limbs even for the mirror therapy. Moseley made the leap that these people might build up their motor maps until they could move their limbs, through imagination alone.

He encouraged his patients to just imagine their limbs were moving. His hope was neuronal pathways would begin to fire in the part of their brains signaling physical movement. To encourage this outcome he also provided pictures of hands and asked his clients to determine very quickly whether the hand was right or left.

This exercise is known to stimulate the motor cortex. Finally patients were shown hands, "…in various positions and asked to imagine them for fifteen minutes three times a day."[11]

After practicing with visualizations like these the patients then undertook the mirror box therapy. This time after twelve weeks pain significantly reduced in some and completely receded in others.

Experiments of scientists like Ramachandran and Moseley prove we can fool our brains into creating desired and measurable physiological change. From that change grows new behaviors. Those new behaviors encourage the new attitudes; those new attitudes lead to increased healthier behavior. However, as deeply felt as the tremors of these exciting experiments are, yet another level of fascinating knowledge opened up.

The stunning work of neuroscientist Alvaro Pascual-Leone, Chief of Beth Israel Deaconess Medical Center, part of Harvard's Medical School, provides an excellent example of another way of creating physiological change: creating those changes using nothing but imagination.

---

[11] Doidge, op. cit., p. 194.

Pascual-Leone devised a brilliantly elegant experiment to demonstrate that our physical actions help determine, influence and create the physical shape of our brains. Even more startling, the same experiment proves that even imagining a physical action determines, influences and creates exactly the same physical changes in our brains as if the action had been physically executed.

Following an intuition of his hero, nineteenth century Nobel laureate Santiago Ramon y Cajal, Pascual-Leone is the first scientist to use TMS or Transcranial Magnetic Stimulation to show the physical map of the brain. Using TMS Pascual-Leone mapped the physical structure of the brain creating visual representations of neural pathways. This machine map indicated where and how much neuronal activity fired during physical movements. His elegant experiment involved such mapping in response to playing piano.

Pascual-Leone gathered a group of subjects who had no previous training in playing piano. He then divided this group into two parts. He showed both groups the same piece of sheet music, demonstrated how to place fingers properly on the piano keys and ensured they heard the music.

The first group played piano for two hours daily for five days sitting at a piano and pressing keys. The second group imagined playing, right down to the finger movements, and the imagined sounds of the notes two hours daily for five days. TMS mapped both groups before, during and after each practice as well as before and after the entire experiment.

Pacual-Leone found similar brain map changes in both groups at the end of the trial time. In other words, imagining playing the piano had induced the same physical changes in brain structure as physically playing the piano!

Piano expertise as calculated by a computer judge included technical competency as well as tone, touch and other areas of artistry. The conclusions clearly demonstrated the group who imagined their practice ran only slightly behind the group who had moved their fingers on real keys. The difference measured at about two-fifths.

When the imagination group finally sat at a real piano they mimicked exactly the same abilities as the other group, in other words they caught up, after only two hours of actual piano time. They matched precisely their manually experienced counterparts in half time! Since the neural pathways needed to play piano had been excited and fired through their imaginations once their fingers touched physical keys they mastered it in quick time.

Imagining created the same structural brain changes as the piano players using physical keys had created. Imagining the piece prepared the brain to make the leap into physical proficiency with greater ease. In other words, mental or imaginative practice alone caused the same physical changes in their brain's neuronal pathways as physical actions.

We can and do change our brains simply by imagining. As multiple experiments have now shown, imagining an act and performing it ignite the same areas of brain pathways. We imagine ourselves into being proficient, say at piano. That act of imagination, truly an act of faking it until you make it, provides exercise for brain pathways that once strengthened provide support real change in our brains, our selves and our lives.

Imagination and Medicine Buddha Meditation

Once brain pathways have been exercised enough in imagination it becomes easier and easier to glide into behavior which follows those neural pathways. For instance, if we imagine ourselves sitting serenely like the Medicine Buddha, offering love symbolized by his open right palm, neuroscience states it becomes easier and easier to chose attitudes and behaviors that match such a visualization. Since the neural pathways for serenity and caring have been exercised frequently during meditation sessions, those brain pathways become the natural conduits of our state of mind, which then guide our behavior in daily life.

The meditation on Medicine Buddha compels us, by returning to the visual imagining of his serenity and openhanded generosity, to exercise the neural pathways of calm serenity and abiding generosity. Eventually we have the neural strength to live our lives even under crisis with an increased sense of serenity, calm and openhandedness. We know now how and why such meditation practice assists us in behaving with increased calm and serenity under all circumstances.

Is that all? Is that all we find in Medicine Buddha practice, a simple gazing and sounding to help create change in our brains and then our lives? The answer is no. Two more significant aspects of Tantric meditation practice parallel what we learn from neuroscience. These aspects involve our personalities directly.

As students of meditation we begin our visualization practice by seeing the figure outside of our body and slightly higher in space in front of us. The picture remains a little above eye level where we gently let our eyes rest upon it, or alternatively gaze and glance away.

This is called "Front Arising Yoga." The word yoga means "to yoke" and generally, since the syllable "Ga" means "God" the whole refers to yoking to God. Thus practicing such a tantric meditation as Medicine Buddha implies a search for what is holy, what transcends our usual daily experience.

In Front Arising Yoga the meditator sees the figure of Medicine Buddha outside the boundaries of her body. As we notice through neuroscience such as Doidge's experience with Ramachandran and the tabletop tapping experiment, those boundaries are not as rigid or solid as we might have believed.

Vajrayana Tantra includes the truth of this porousness of boundaries by including a second practice, Self Arising Yoga. In Self Arising Yoga the meditator herself becomes Medicine Buddha. By replacing all parts of her body with that of the figure of Medicine Buddha, she herself becomes for the duration of the meditation Medicine Buddha. Clearly this practice, exercised over time, enlarges the psychic space, the felt sense of self to include a patient, serene, faith filled, confident, and capable self, the self of Medicine Buddha.

We have explored some of the parallel experiments and results in neuroscience and in the exercises of

Vajrayana Tantra on a general level. However, how do we address that notion, central to meditation practice, of self? Does neuroscience offer any understanding that may open our minds about our concept of self? The answer is yes. Mirror Neurons.

Mirror Neurons: Self and Others

Up to this point we have fixed our gaze on how what happens in Medicine Buddha practice promotes neuronal change, shifts the shape of our brains and provides a platform from which we may with enough practice begin to alter our behavior. Now we look at the inspiration behind much of Western medicine and much of Tantric meditation practice: the relief from suffering or pain.

Buddhism posits as one of its core tenets that when we see others in pain, we ourselves feel pain. Until very recently this understanding demanded faith: reliance upon one's teachers, who have the experience that giving helps the giver more than the receiver, or upon the texts which state that the pain of others must be taken as seriously as one's own. Happily, neuroscience now explains why when we see others in pain, we register the pain in ourselves.

A caveat may be needed here: not all humans are gifted in this way. Extensive research on Psychopaths confirms they lack the ability to feel what others are feeling. For much of the rest of humanity however, this empathy no longer sits as a longed for or regrettably missed moral characteristic, endowed at birth or not by mysterious forces.

In his delightful book, Mirroring People, Marco Iacoboni explains, "For the past 150 years or so…no one could begin to explain how it is that we know what others are doing, thinking and feeling."[12]

Of course, Psychotherapy and Philosophy refer to this idea as Theory of Mind. For our purposes we restrict

---

[12]M. Iacoboni, Mirroring People,)New York, New York Farrar, Straus and Giroux, 2008) p.4

ourselves to neuroscience and its discoveries of how we feel what others experience.

A group of cells aptly called Mirror Neurons positioned at the front of the brain navigate our every day experiences, helping us connect to each other. Mirror Neurons allow us to believe we know, and indeed we can believe we know from results in neuroscience, what others are doing, feeling and experiencing.

Through responses to many experiments on monkeys, scientists recognized that, "…motor cells could fire merely at the perception of somebody else's actions, with no motor action involved at all."[13]

Those motor cells are called mirror neurons. Experiment after experiment proves, "…(that) a subset of cells in our brains—the mirror neurons—fire when an individual kicks a soccer ball, sees a ball being kicked, hears a ball being kicked and even just says or hears the word "kick" leads to amazing consequences and new understandings."[14]

---

[13]Ibid. p.11
[14]Ibid. p.12

In a mirror like statement to the Tibetan belief, and the belief of all world religions about compassion, Iacoboni states, "When we see someone else suffering or in pain, mirror neurons help us to read her or his facial expression and actually make us feel the suffering or pain of the other person."[15]

Mirror neurons light up in response to the actions of others. This explains why when we watch sports on TV we see many "reaction shots" that is, the camera's pick up of the faces and body language of fans in the stands with their highly emotional reactions. Again, Iacoboni states unequivocally, "These shots are effective television because our mirror neurons make sure that by seeing these emotions, we share them."[16]

Consider what this means. Western science's latest discoveries support the central organizing principle of Buddhist meditation rising from one of Buddhism's core tenets: when we see suffering in others, we ourselves experience some suffering. The reverse obviously works as

---

[15]Ibid. p. 5
[16]Ibid. p.5

well: by literally setting our sights on a figure of calm serenity and loving generosity we ourselves experience an increase in neuronal activity accompanying such attitudes.

While Medicine Buddha Tantra has provided relief to untold numbers of people across the centuries the requisite for that relief has been faith in Medicine Buddha, faith in the practice, faith in one's teacher. In other words, the desired results depended upon the strength of one's faith.

Those of us whose faith wavers now may rely on science: we know our brains change. We know our brains, and our sense of self, changes with every activity in which we engage, so shifting activities to include meditation upon Medicine Buddha helps provide relief from the suffering of pain. We continue our exploration on how this works.

Phantom Emotional Pain

Ramachandran believes our brains produce phantom pain of a physical kind. It is a small step to believe our brains produce phantom pain of an emotional kind as well. Every day countless human hours, minutes and seconds are wasted in the useless devotion to phantom pain: not to release it, but to increase it! So many people do not know that focusing on the emotional hurts, the pains inflicted by others and by life, must be let go of, not out of some sense of forgiveness but for oneself.

If a person is able to truly let go of the grave injustices life sometimes inflicts, that shows a great heart. For those of us who are farther behind in our development, those of us who increase our suffering by clinging to the pains of the past, knowing about neuronal pathways may inspire us to change the focus.

Emotional pains are as real as any physical pain arising from a brain that believes a severed limb still clings to the body. The pain from remembered and emotional experiences is as real to the person experiencing them as the pain of a phantom limb to the amputee.

For instance every day repetitious thoughts stubbornly cycle through, on some days adding to an already approaching attitude of gloom or despair. Those thoughts, those memories are phantoms just as surely as the amputated limbs on the body of an amputee. Yet the suffering is as real. Through applying awareness and with dedicated efforts these thoughts can be changed from their old and negative groove into new pathways describing new positive thoughts.

For those of us working with the more usual kinds of patterning than with physical phantom limbs, simply refocusing our brains to a positive image, for instance Medicine Buddha, helps to relocate our attention in a positive way.

As we refocus with intention we change the neuronal pathways of our previously negative mind habits into increased joy and happiness. This is a measurable, material, structural change. Norman Doidge explains, "Everything your 'immaterial" mind imagines leaves material traces. Each thought alters the physical state of your brain synapses at a microscopic level…while we have yet to understand exactly how thoughts actually change brain structure, it is now clear that they do…" [17]

If you have some phantom emotional pain, a simple way that takes nothing more than dedication, persistence and patience to release inner tension goes like this. Whenever you find yourself remembering a pain, an emotional hurt, bring yourself, your mind and awareness down to your feet. Right now try it. Wherever your feet hit the surface, be it the rung of a chair, the floor, your shoes or socks, bring your awareness to your feet. Now go up through your body slowly and consistently reminding yourself, "I am here now. I feel well. I am positive and healthy right now." This may be practiced anywhere throughout the day until you can get back to your meditation mat or chair. Once in meditation, the focus upon Medicine Buddha in his confidence, serenity and lack of fear increases substantially your ability to let go.

What you are doing is rewiring your brain. Eventually instead of going toward the memory with its pain, a new neuronal pathway will, with practice, become

---

[17] Doidge, op. cit., p.214

a highway of neuronal strength taking your thoughts towards awareness of well being in the present moment. In time you will no longer register the pain, even if now and again the memory of the original event rises to mind.

A subtle but important point lies within the experiment of V.S. Ramachandran. That is, the sensory details the brain picks up right now can and will override many of the neuronal pathways, even those that are well developed. This is the neuronal secret behind the cliché, "Be Here Now."

<u>Pain, Fear and Focusing Elsewhere</u>

Namgyal Rinpoche usually referred to himself as "this being." I never understood exactly why but that was the way it was. He sat one day with his hands on his khaki kneed pants and stated, "This being visited the Dentist and had several teeth pulled, and several fixed, without anesthetic." He eyeballed the room full of students for emphasis.

Nothing motivates human exploration like the province of pain and how to avoid it. To listen then to someone declare a pain free dental experience or to watch a yogi insert needles under his fingernails without demonstrating any discomfort leaves us with challenging inquiries into the nature of pain.

When I work with clients in my Psychotherapy practice who experience on-going physical pain or when as a meditation teacher someone asks about pain, I've found a helpful question. That is, "Where is the border between physical pain and fear?"

Fear, a useful ally when we need immediate detailed information about our bodies and the environment, becomes a rosary of dread when linked to physical pain. Sufferers rotate an ugly carousel of endless thoughts rising from fear: when will the pain return? Is the pain getting stronger? Will it be worse than before? In response to these thoughts or perhaps as a biochemical impetus to the formation of such torturous patterns of thought, fear clamps muscles on subtle or broad levels. This restricts or prevents the flow of blood, oxygen and lymph required for our bodies to feel better.

Whenever meditators successfully focus on the present moment, with little fear, the pain becomes just that: pain, in this moment. This allows relaxation and relaxation leads to deeper breath so oxygen, blood and lymph flow more easily. How?

Part of the answer comes from another question: if you know the pain you are in will not increase, will in fact decrease, can you acclimatize to it more easily?

Admittedly this takes much training. Personally I ask for anesthetic whenever my teeth need more than a cleaning and I'm grateful for the person hours, ingenuity and compassion that encourage ever more refined understanding of pain and relief from pain.

My own life has offered ample opportunity for healing from physical and emotional pain and for inquiry into their differences.

I was born in 1952 when it was the fashion to remove newborns from their mothers' warm body and reassuring heart beat and put them in solitary. This experience alerts the newborn brain to abandonment, signaling imminent death so if the baby's system is not flooded, as most were at the time, with drugs intended to ease mother's trial in giving birth, the newborn cries piteously and endlessly until sleep.

The 1950's style of child rearing in many places, including my working class home, revolved around a notion of spoiling the baby, the toddler or growing child. Parents of the day perceived their offspring as being very like apples, subject to rot with too much handling. Clean, dry and fed was the jingle, then lie the baby down to sleep or presumably to amuse herself.

My mother's undiagnosed mental fractures led to frequent severe beatings with a leather belt accompanied by violent verbal abuse in line with her understanding of child raising: spare the rod and spoil the child.

My older brother's psychic distortions led him to use me sexually and what was more damaging to humiliate and degrade me as he did so.

I broke reins and fled in the middle of one September night, hitchhiking out of Toronto on a dream of reaching a friend in Edmonton. It was 1968. The Summer of Love had just ended. Nothing could go wrong, right?

I got into the car of my own will. The two men, Al and Gary inside were escaped convicts. They would keep me hostage, make me witness to their murder of a man with a sawed-off shot gun, rape me, tie me to a chair and torture me with burns, bites, slaps and verbal abuse.

In 1993 having successfully freed myself of that past enough to have achieved my graduate degrees, to be teaching at a college, to be recently re-wed and to be raising my son into a wonderful man, I approached the Ontario Board for Compensation to Victims of Crime.

I had to provide enough evidence to convince an adjudicator my story was true. Part of the criteria was to be examined by a Psychiatrist.

I sat sobbing in Dr. Roger's office as I relayed the deepest parts of that journey at 16 years old. He held up his hand, offering me Kleenex with the other.

"We don't see this..." he began.

"Does this mean you don't believe me?"

"Oh, no, I believe you, it's just that we don't know how you've done this. You should be under Doctor's care and in and out of hospitals for the rest of your life. Instead you are not only functioning, you're high functioning."

I was awarded a sum of money. That money told me Dr. Rogers, the adjudicator and everyone who learned this part of my life understood I'd been subject to severe violence. What no one understood was how I had healed.

When I returned in September of 1968 from those days, I was a mess. Within a year Namgyal Rinpoche entered my life.

What he offered among the cornucopia of healing modalities at his command, from bio-energetics, to art therapy, from Mandala therapy to travel through Europe, Asia and Australia, from meditation retreat where the focus was Tantric meditation to explorations in deep sea diving, was most of all hope.

I began meditating upon the various figures offered through Tibetan Vajrayana Tantra meditation beginning with Chen Rezig while in an intensive three month long retreat in New Zealand in 1972.

For each Wong we received, either from him or from His Holiness Chogyam Rinpoche through His Holiness Sakya Trizen, Namgyal Rinpoche made it clear we must complete 108 thousand repetitions. It was our responsibility to use the great tools of healing showered upon us by the Tibetan Masters and by Namgyal's western influences: Alexander Lowen, Freud, Art Therapy,

Western Mysteries including Astrology, Tarot, as well as Namgyal himself.

He believed in the union of East and West, in the inherent complementarity of consciousness. He was a scientist of Consciousness and he extolled the virtues of self-discovery. "Don't take my word for it; find out for yourselves."

So I did, experimenting with many of the modalities he blessed us with, as well as some from outside his realm. I worked. I worked at every exercise that kept my body inching toward a tiny bit more ease. I meditated with devotion on the hundreds of thousands of visualizations and mantras. I meditated because I had no choice and I meditated because every time I did, I felt that small bit closer to something I yearned toward. And I meditated because as long as I did, I wasn't paying attention to the body depression and deep anxiety that continued to flood out of those three days in the Ontario north.

<u>Moscowitz Demonstrates Pain and Refocusing</u>

Norman Doidge's latest book, <u>The Brain's Way of</u>
<u>Healing, Remarkable Discoveries and Recoveries from the</u>

Frontiers of Neuroplasticity, features in the first chapter the remarkable experiences of Dr. Moscowitz.

Dr. Michael Moskowitz's list of professional and scholarly accomplishments demonstrates both his academic acumen and his dedication to a goal. A psychiatrist, he sat on the examination council for the American Board of Pain Medicine (helping to set exams for doctors in pain medicine); is a former chair of the Education Committee of the American Academy of Pain Medicine and holds an advanced psychiatric fellowship in psychosomatic medicine. Not someone you might take as interested in Eastern or out of bounds natural medicine.

After a severe boating accident when the pain in his neck sent him to rock bottom in his fifty-seventh year, he researched neuroplasticity and its relation to pain and pain management arriving at an elegant and clear understanding. Acute pain signals that we must do something immediately and where the doing needs to take place. However, acute pain sometimes ignites plasticity in such a way that our brain keeps interpreting "pain is present" even after the pain has diminished. This is called Neuropathic pain.

Remember the axiom "neurons that fire together wire together." Recall how the neurons in our brains may start out as tiny foot paths but with dedicated thoughts and emotions in one direction, more neurons fire, wiring together and creating larger and larger pathways for that same thought, those same emotions. Thus it was "…the more often Moscowitz felt twinges of neck pain, the more easily his brain's neurons recognized it, and the more intense it got. The name for this well-documented neuroplastic process is wind-up pain, because the more the receptors in the pain system fired, the more sensitive they became."[18]

Moscowitz figured a way around the constant firing of his brain. He first clarified some of his thoughts around his pain. He recognized his thoughts included an expectation of pain in the future. His research made him know "…these expectations play a major role in the level of pain we will feel."[19] This psychiatrist, pain specialist and now neuroscience researcher realized his thoughts

---

[18] N. Doidge, The Brain's Way of Healing, (New York, New York, Penguin Group, 2014) p.12
[19] Ibid, p. 11

about the future, and the fear contained in those thoughts, influenced how much pain his brain registered.

Moscowitz decided to turn the axiom of neurons firing together wiring together on its head. "Neurons that fire apart, wire apart" became his guiding credo. As Doidge recounts, "As he analyzed the areas that fire in chronic pain he observed that many of those areas also process thoughts, sensations, images, memories, movements, emotions and beliefs—when they are not processing pain. That observation explained why, when we are in pain, we can't concentrate or think well; why we have sensory problems and often can't tolerate certain sounds or light; why we can't move more gracefully; and why we can't control our emotions very well and become irritable and have emotional outbursts. The areas that regulate these activities have been hijacked to process the pain signal."[20]

Then Moscowitz put his theory to test. He drew maps of the brain and dedicated himself to visualizing those maps every time he got an attack of pain, to remind himself the brain really can change.

_____

[20] Ibid, p. 11-12

Here we find a Western Psychiatrist, trained in pain as a specialty applying the same repeat, repeat and repeat again formula passed down from religious schools from many traditions. Christians believe in repeating rosaries to overcome and help balance the effects of emotional pain, Tantric Meditation masters believe in repeating visualizations and mantras for refuge from physical and mental or emotional pain as well as for promoting health and balance. The only difference may be that up until now schools of religious thought and practice have required faith while neuroscience tells us what our brains are doing and why repeating visualizations, mantras and prayers works to reduce pain.

Moscowitz' return to a pain free life took months, but it did happen. Doidge reports, "By six weeks, the pain between his shoulders in his back and near his shoulder blades had completely disappeared, never to return. By four months, he was having his first totally pain-free periods throughout his neck. And within a year he was almost always pain free..."[21]

---

[21]Ibid., p.15.

Moscowitz then took what he knew back into the world he knew, where people with pain turned to him for help. He had a new way to offer them relief based on his own truth.

Another account from Moscowitz involves a patient of his, Jan. A nurse on the cardiac ward, Jan had been helping her patient when a complicated situation devolved. "Suddenly Jan was supporting the full weight of nearly three hundred pounds..."[22] She heard a sound like "...a rubber band snapping..." and she "...felt something inside me break."[23]

All five of her low back discs were damaged leading to excruciating pain that ruined her life. In her words, "I couldn't even watch TV or read because on top of the pain the drugs I took put me in a grey zone. There was no reason to live..."[24] By the time she got to Moscowitz she had been disabled with chronic pain for a decade."[25] Tragically, thousands of others suffer in the same way.

---

[22]Ibid., p. 16.
[23]Ibid., p.16.
[24] Ibid, p. 16
[25] Ibid, p. 17

By the time Moscowitz and Jan met, Moscowitz had some real help to impart. He showed Jan his own three drawings of the brain, "…and told her she had to be more relentless than the pain in focusing on them."[26]

Moscowitz went one step further, "He urged her to hold on to the thought that if her brain looked like the no-pain picture, she couldn't have any pain."[27] This was the mantra accompanying the visual.

Jan was a model patient. From a meditation point of view she was a model practitioner. Instead of looking at the pictures throughout the day, a glance at a time as Moscowitz suggested, she took it upon herself to look at the pictures continually. In three weeks she experienced a couple of minutes a day without chronic pain. By the fourth week "…the pain-free periods were up to fifteen minutes to half an hour."[28]

These results are staggering, considering how traditional western medicine considers back pain almost untreatable except with drugs. Moscowitz and Jan Sandin provide hope for all who suffer from physical pain that by

---

[26] Ibid, p. 17
[27] Ibid, p. 17
[28] Ibid, p. 18

refocusing thought, relief is possible. With their courage and sheer relentlessness they reshaped the way we contemplate pain in our bodies.

Fascinating to note these two achieved their results without a religious framework but deeply dependent upon faith. They found a way to rewire their brains using a simple drawing of the brain itself.

When we consider the baroque example of even so dressed down an example of Tantric iconography as Medicine Buddha we must ask whether the details count? Does pain relief arrive more quickly when the contemplation object is Medicine Buddha as opposed to simple brain drawings? Or does the outcome depend upon sheer stubborn refusal to give up and a smidgeon of faith?

Medicine Buddha

Although many forms of visualization exist and many are helpful, even drawings of our brain, as Moscowitz demonstrated, may provide the refocusing needed to change our brains and relieve pain.

Without intention of replacing any of the highly religious, even mystical possibilities associated with meditation upon Medicine Buddha, it is important to look at some of the details offered in this visualization to see what Western science has to tell us.

His robes, unlike the robes of most deities in the Tibetan panoply, signify the earth. The simple orange and brown robes of a monk indicate how much Medicine Buddha connects with the earth in a simple and direct way. The saffron color provides a balance to the blue by offering the opposite vibration.

Namgyal Rinpoche suggested the blue and orange combination evokes a flame, such as the flame of vital force within the mitochondria of each cell of our bodies. Thought of in this way, the figure heralds to the individual cells of our bodies in the language of color.

His right hand rests comfortably on his right knee. If you practice in this posture you will find the only way to achieve it is to keep your spine at a comfortable but straight angle. The outstretched palm pointing toward the world releases the energy from the chakra in the middle of Medicine Buddha's palm, energy flowing outward to ease the suffering of the world.

We absorb in this detail a sense of a superior being as one who gives, who turns toward the suffering. This is one meaning of Tantra: to be with the suffering. And in the case of Moscowitz and Sandin this turning toward the suffering and paying attention to the brain demonstrates how powerful this may be.

Notice the meditator herself accepts the help first, feels the balm of healing first and only then offers it. This insight was offered to me in personal interview with the deceased Lama Yogi Kalsang Rinpoche.

Next we focus on the flower in his right hand. This herb, called the King of Medicines produces all cures. It is the Arura Plant in Tibetan, also known as Cherubic Myrobalan. From www.henriettes-herb.com we read, " In India and China, where the species are indigenous, the fruit is highly valued for almost every ill that flesh is heir to."

The mind is a powerful tool and when we project onto a medicine that it will heal us, then we are often correct! Consider the placebo effect, which tallies at about 50% relief from symptoms with ingredients that are known to have no healing power at all. Here in the Medicine Buddha depiction, a fruit that has healing power shows up in the picture of an elevated Medicine Healer, as the signature healing fruit of all time. Add the power of human consciousness to believe in good faith and a strong element of health is certainly indicated.

The bowl in Medicine Buddha's lap contains 'the nectar of the Gods' which heals all disease. Clearly the entire picture offers the faithful a path to release from suffering.

At this point some understanding needs to be clarified. The meditation on Medicine Buddha is not a cure all for all disease or any disease. It is never to be undertaken rather than following a doctor's advice, be that doctor Tibetan or Western. The Medicine Buddha teachings relate most strongly to the three poisons in which humans are believed by Buddhists to be steeped: hatred, greed and delusion. It is our task so the Buddhist belief goes to transmute these three poisons to their beneficial counterparts: discriminating wisdom, faith and intuitive perception.

It remains clear, however, that distracting one's focus from pain, suffering and disease proves, through meditation experience as well as now through neuroscience, to reduce the messages of pain, suffering and disease in favor of wherever the mind does focus.

A lovely tool for considering this switch in focus comes to us from the children's program "Sesame Street." Decades ago as I watched with my young son, an animated skit came on in which the tv screen filled with the image of a single insect. In the background voices sang in a lovely lilt, "That's about the size, where you put your eyes, that's about the size of it." Some light glimmered my mind into awareness and I paid closer attention.

The next shot was of the insect but included the twig the insect sat upon with the same little song in the background. Next shot, the insect, twig and branch, the next included the yard, the insect, twig branch and tree occupied, then the city block, the town, county, state, country and out to a shot of the entire planet all the while with the sweet song and its simple wisdom flowing. Finally the Universes and that's about the size of it!

I have used this little ditty and the shifting screens to help meditation students grasp how powerful our brains are and how important it is that we practice switching up and letting go. I am still humbly moved by the power of that television show and how its wisdom passed sweetly along to so many little minds and hearts.

In 1977 Namgyal Rinpoche bestowed the Medicine Buddha Wong in the living room of his rented villa in Chania. It is my belief the quality and power of the transmission teacher, which depends also on the mystery of connection, or not, with the individual student, defines what happens during the Wong. As the Teacher enters into the actual brain patterns of the main player of the Wong, in this case Medicine Buddha, he offers to students the potential for their individual brains to match, to hook up as it were, to learn the pathways that express this greater experience. In this way the teacher is, for the student the beloved, respected, revered person deserving of every moment of dedication.

While it is true some masters of transmission are worthy of this kind of veneration, it is also true that some, while capable of transmission in the moments of the Wong, remain humanly flawed and therefore not worthy of the unquestioning devotion all masters speak of as the students' obligation.

Namgyal Rinpoche also gave instructions for the meditation on Medicine Buddha in which we were to imagine millions upon millions of exact replicas of Medicine Buddha all around, some as small as a mustard seed and some as large as the sky.

It brought to my mind a practice he had given a few years earlier. While in meditation retreat (no phones, letters, no tv, no electronic devices, and strict silence at all times) he suggested a practice of incrementally decreasing the size of the visualization, down to the measurement of a mustard seed (the traditional description for this exercise) while maintaining all the details, then incrementally blowing the visualization up to fill the sky, the universe and beyond.

Practice with this was significantly more satisfying to me than the usual, such that of all the meditation exercises he offered, this one remains in my memory as extremely powerful and somehow very helpful in creating a sense of inner balance and emotional stability. I came to believe this exercise might help increase my perspective and bring it more into balance.

With my Western habit of questioning I wanted to know why it worked.

Barbie Dolls, Neuroscience and A Path From the Past

Traditionally scientists thought the size of objects as we perceive them, came from somewhere in our eyes, from "…the combination of information from a variety of visual and oculomotor cues."[29]. Yet recent research demonstrates our perception, based on our perceived body size, rules how we estimate an object's distance from our body or size by comparison.

These researchers, van der Hoort, Guterstam and Ehrsson took on the main task of finding out whether our sense of the size of our bodies has any effect on how we perceive the size of objects. The answer, for those who enjoy the last chapter first, is yes. Our perception of the size of our bodies directly impacts our perception of distance and size of objects, whether they are near or far, large or small.

The scientists asked volunteers to lie on a bed with cameras angled toward a bed opposite them. The cameras served as another set of eyes for the volunteers. On the bed opposite lay a Barbie doll. In a set of experiments known as "body swap illusion," researchers built upon the simple

---

[29] Bjorn van der Hoort, Arvid Guterstam, H. Henrik Ehrsson, May 25, 2011, DOI:10:1371/journal/pone/0020195 PLOS one.

experience of those like Dr. Norman Doidge as cited earlier. We recall his hand and the table top merged body maps as demonstrated by Dr. Ramachandran.

Work on the "Body Swap Illusion" continued until researchers found the whole body might be sensed through another's whole body! The abstract for an article in the online site PLOS ONE puts it this way "Here we report a perceptual illusion of body-swapping that addresses directly this issue. Manipulation of the visual perspective, in combination with the receipt of correlated multisensory information from the body was sufficient to trigger the illusion that another person's body or an artificial body was one's own. This effect was so strong that people could experience being in another person's body when facing their own body and shaking hands with it. Our results are of fundamental importance because they identify the perceptual processes that produce the feeling of ownership of one's body."[30]

Notice carefully what is said, "…people could experience being in another person's body when facing

---

[30] Valeria Petkova, H. Henrik Ehrsson, "If I Were You: Perceptual Illusion of Body Swapping" December 3, 2008, DOI:10:13711/Journal.pone.0003832

their own body and shaking hands with it." We can have the perception of occupying an alternate angle and dimension in space strongly enough to experience shaking our own hand!

The Barbie Doll experiments took the situation a bit farther. Through visual/tactile sight, eg volunteers watched researchers stroking the arms or legs of the Barbie doll, scientists encouraged volunteers to experience themselves to be the size of the doll on the bed opposite. As measured through carefully controlled questions after the experiments, volunteers acknowledged they felt the stimulation on their own legs, when Barbie's legs were touched.

First the scientists established the body-swap experience in the volunteers. Then they measured volunteers' skin-conductance response (SCR) as they cut through the abdomen of the Barbie doll. The volunteers' responses indicated through increases in their skin-conductivity responses they felt strong effects from the cut.

Following these parts of the experience the volunteers, still perceiving themselves as small as the Barbie doll, held or reached for a few common objects like a pencil or another person's regularly sized finger. Then they had to answer a series of questions. Their responses demonstrate that when participants felt themselves to be as small as a Barbie doll, the objects appeared much larger than normal.

Researchers also conducted similar experiments using a much larger than normal human mannequin with the same results. When volunteers perceived themselves to be larger, the common objects and their distance from the volunteers' perceptually larger bodies appeared much smaller and farther away.

The exciting new information rising from such experiments hold promise for a slew of difficult to treat conditions that plague us, such as arthritis, chronic back pain and neuralgia to name a few. By exchanging one's own pain ridden body even temporarily with the pain free body of a substitute our brains learn to rewire out of the repetitive pain signals into other pathways. Something else lies at the heart of this data: a way to perceive ourselves out of the trap of the past.

The Trap of the Past: Meditation and Neuroscience

A meditator sits down to experience Medicine Buddha meditation in the quiet of her meditation place. As the meditation proceeds and the mantra continues, along with the many glances at the beautiful Tangkha she has hung up just above eye level, she notices something else.

Her mind wanders across the past. Not only the moments or days before this meditation, but the moments and days of her entire life! Commercial jingles, movie scenes and scores, advertisements from her childhood, scenes from ten years ago, that time she got caught doing…the emotional upheaval of that…

She steers her mind gently to the present moment and tries to dwell again on Medicine Buddha and the lovely sounds of the mantra. Now it's anger. Why try? This doesn't work anyway. "Even if this meditation stuff works for others, it won't work for me," she thinks. "I might as well get up and…" fill in your favorite or least favorite activity.

The ability to stay gently focused on the present moment takes a mountain of patience and a universe of determination. Nowhere is that more true than when practicing Tantric meditation, the joining with a divine figure for the purposes of release from suffering.

Notice. The meditator falls quickly into "It won't work for me." That's the self-referencing every meditation manual anywhere will sooner or later reveal as the most troublesome part of our life experience.

In Buddhism the term is "No Self." There actually is No Self to which to refer but we insist upon it. We feel from our heads, hearts and bodies that we exist in a particular time/space dimension that is fundamentally solid, and at least for the foreseeable future permanent.

Yet results from Western science's experiments tell us we are neither solid, in the sense of unchanging nor is our perception of ourselves as permanent a reliable one.

First the solid bit. Quantum mechanics tells us the space between the molecules of our bodies outdoes the distance between the planets in our solar system. If you can grasp this, please get in touch with me! I have been teaching this moment as a part of the Sunyata meditation in every meditation for over thirty years and still the mystery of it is all I get. Yet the response from all meditators including myself is that somehow the sense of distance is immensely comforting and relaxing.

When we look at the Barbie doll experiments outlined in the last chapter we see how everything depends upon our perspective or as the creative geniuses at Sesame Street put it, "That's about the size/ where you put your eyes/ that's about the size of it."

When I recollect my experience in strict meditation retreat in New Zealand of enlarging and shrinking the meditation deity I see the same situation. We can and do practice expanding and shrinking ourselves according to experience.

Here's how it works. Someone hurts you. You feel the hurt. Your mind registers the pain, in the way our brains are organized to recognize pain as a signal to stop and get help. However we find ourselves thinking about the same event, the same hurt over and over as though we took comfort from remembering, "Yes, I did get hurt." Every time we recall the emotionally painful event we re-experience the emotional pain. And soon neurons have fired together and wired together.

The trouble is now we build. We build a sense of self, based in that experience. "I am the person to whom…" this event, be it tragedy on the level of accidental death of a loved one, rape, loss of a career, personal accident, so on, happened. That's all we see.

What the meditation of expansion and diminishing helps do is release us from the unhealthy repetition of the identity formed around the hurts. It works in the same way as the Barbie Doll experiments.

The meditator sits (and finds it is somewhat easier to keep a gentle focus when the figure grows and shrinks as she repeats mantras) and the figure upon which she dwells gets larger and larger. Her imagination expands and her imagination of the Medicine Buddha constructs an ever larger deity until the sky and all the universes are filled with only lapis lazuli colored Medicine Buddha, simultaneously each tiny tiny Medicine Buddha and all the sizes in between, cascade around.

On the subtle levels of neural wiring she is practicing the expansion and diminishing of herself. As we have seen from the extraordinary piano experiments conducted by Dr. Pascual-Leone, imagination alone does affect behavior, in this case making it easier and easier to perceive differently about oneself. This freedom to perceive oneself differently, larger and smaller, allows her to consider things from different angles.

After the meditation session she may find herself thinking, "Well, yes I was hurt in that instance. But what about all the times others have helped me?" Or she may find herself considering, "Yes, I was hurt. Have I never hurt others?" and without flagellating, recollect times when she hurt someone.

The capacity to turn the angle around, to consider situations from larger and smaller perspectives flows more naturally after the practice of stretching and shrinking visualized figures. The stretching and shrinking wire together pathways that are useful when it comes to releasing a sense of self from the myriad moments of pain and disruption from the past.

Some researchers believe our thoughts tend toward the negative, fear and aversion because those two experiences helped steer us away from death. Over centuries the sense of fear alerted us to instantly recognize details and determine whether to flee or fight. The same with aversion: those berries made someone sick last time. Thus our brains are wired for those two expressions.

When we ruminate we tend therefore to dwell upon the experiences that provoked fear or aversion. The trouble is our brain wiring that worked so well in the ancient past merely serves to bring us a distorted view of ourselves at this point in time. Having no immediate need of the same levels of fear and aversion, our brains nonetheless continue to measure emotional hurts and losses with the same stick of fear and aversion. Tantric Meditation helps release us from the cycle of self referencing through the narrow lens of terror, hurt, and pain to build a renewed and more flexible sense of self through focus on the present and focus on the positive whether past, present or future.

Forward From Here

Namgyal Rinpoche passed from this life in October 2003 just prior to the moment Neuroscience grabbed center stage in Western and global science. He passed but his connection with human advances and the creativity of minds toward healing was not finished.

In the peculiar way time occasionally has of revealing its folds I was given a gift and, as I felt it, encouragement toward completing this small book when I first opened Norman Doidge's second boon on Neuroscience and healing called <u>The Brain's Way of Healing.</u> I split the fresh, stiff spine of the book, glancing at the list of chapter headings and saw Chapter Six "A Blind Man Learns to See: Using Feldenkrais, Buddhist and Other Neuroplastic Methods."[31] Doidge had listed Buddhist healing technologies, along with those of Moshe Feldenkrais as Neuroplasticity.

I turned to p. 197 interested in the Buddhist part and took a fast gasp of breath at the first two words, a name: David Webber.

Surely this could not be the same David Webber I recall from one of those magical moments of travels with Namgyal? It was in Italy, at a monastery called Santa Tecla, atop a small mountain near Assissi. We had an early afternoon break from the two classes and evening Wong schedule Namgyal generously provided.

My tent provided no escape from the oppressive heat bearing down as afternoon storm clouds gathered for

---

[31] N.Doidge, <u>The Brain's Way of Healing,</u> (New York, New York, Penguin Group, 2014) Contents

their almost daily intense showers. I wandered into the cool of the monastery, walked along the aisle of beds in the men's section and, seeing no one around, lay down on one of the single beds.

Early afternoon light filtered through the openings that served as windows. The concrete floor and walls provided welcome relief from the weighty humidity outside. David Webber walked in. He stood smiling, his beautiful green eyes dominant in his kind face.

"Would you like a massage?" he asked. To my hesitation he assured me, "Just a massage." His voice was so kind and sincere I allowed my usual defensiveness to drop a little.

He began with my hand and was working on my arm when a couple of the other travellers, men from our group, walked in.

"What's going on?" one asked cheerfully.

"Just massaging Charlene."

"Sounds like a good idea."

As these young men surrounded my prone body, I breathed in and made a conscious decision to accept this experience, in spite of the gripping nerves that held taut inside of me for reasons I did not yet remember.

Before long six men were massaging my body, arms, legs, hands, feet, shoulders, neck and face, with respect and care. I believe this experience, initiated spontaneously by David, helped remove old wiring and begin the process of new, healthier wiring toward men.

Here in Norman Doidge's book the heart-wrenching and inspirational story of David's progress from debilitating illness and terrifying pain to real health, rose to join hands with our personal past. The mixed sensations of disbelief and incredulity continued as I read on.

David, Doidge reports, had asked Namgyal Rinpoche for his advice on healing David's particular plight. The book almost dropped from my hands. My teacher's wisdom shone from the pages of this amazing book on Neuroplasticity!

I suppose in retrospect this may not be such a large synchronicity to others. However my teacher's presence in my life, including the particular experience led by David on that day in Assisi Italy so many years ago streaming with the world renowned research and power of writing by

Norman Doidge created a confluence of optimism within. I felt a surge of confidence my desire to write this small book was on the right track.

Conclusions

No conclusions of a hard and fast nature come with this book although I hope further research into Vajrayana Tantra meditation techniques and their affect on our brains will yield excellent results. It is however easy to see that with what we know from Neuroscience about how our brains work the application of focus and concentration upon figures and mantras, prayers and invocations light positive and very healing circuitry within our neural pathways.

It seems ancient techniques and frontier-blasting discoveries now cooperate to offer a dynamic new approach to healing.

I've heard it said many times, often with a tone of slight regret, we don't come into this life with a manual of instructions. Like you, I've also heard people say we need an instruction manual for how our consciousness works.

While Neuroscience does not address the rather large scope of Consciousness but satisfies itself with the realm of what is physically evident in the brain, still, results spill over. As we learn to apply the understanding "neurons that fire together/wire together" the implications of living with more clarity, more joy, and more non-clinging awareness (the three qualities Namgyal Rinpoche said arose with spiritual progress), strengthens.

As we rewire emotional and physical pain from the past, focusing and strengthening our pathways toward the present moment, we find our lives in an enriched way.

I believe no path, no wisdom will change the nature of this dimension. It is one of duality, conflict and challenge. The mark of maturity and stability is the capacity to rebound to a center focus of wellbeing, amidst the turmoil and sometimes tragedies of life.

We are in an extraordinarily abundant historic period where the roads of the past meet present day insights; where traditions from distance places mingle with the relatively new world's culture. The confluence of these streams of human knowledge offers vast potential for healing and the release from suffering. May it be so for you, and for all sentient life!

<u>Appendix One: Visualization of Ideal Self</u>

A brief description of Visualization may be helpful here.

First find a quiet, comfortable place where you may lie

down, fully stretched out.

Let your breath find a natural rhythm and dwell for several moments on what is positive and bright in your world. Let yourself feel in your body the response to these positive thoughts.

Now picture another you, joined seamlessly at the soles of your feet. This you embodies everything you aspire toward: compassionate, patient, intelligent, full of humor and optimism, good health in body, speech and mind and as many attributes such as these as you can recall. Now watch as the figure becomes a peach color, full of light that spreads slightly beyond its boundaries.

Rest with the ideal for several moments, then be sure to dissolve the figure and its surroundings before you sit up slowly. Rest in a sitting posture for a few minutes before leaving.

Glossary

1. Abhiseka: annointing, consecration, inauguration (as

king) the inclusion of the word "king" in this definition taken from the Pali-English Dictionary, (edited by T.W. Rhys Davids and William Stede, published by the Pali Text Society, Oxford England 1999) indicates the elevated or superior quality of the experience of being annointed or consecrated during the initiation ceremony known as Wong, or Wongkur

1. Vehicle or Path: three vehicles or Paths comprise Tibetan Buddhism: the Hinayana or lesser path, the Mahayana or Greater Path and the Vajrayana or Higher or Diamond Path. The paths indicate different methods for reaching higher states of consciousness

1. His Holiness Chogyam Rinpoche

1. His Holiness Sakya Trizen : His Holiness is the head of the Sakya Sect of Tibetan Buddhism. Heads of Sects are generally recognized from one lifetime to another by a group of elders. The Tibetan Buddhist system is extremely hierarchical and the "recognition" of a head may be as much politically based as mystically inspired

1. Lung: word meaning the oral transmission, sometimes including the history given during the Wong or Wongkur ceremony of initiation aka empowerment

1. Mantra: "There are seven major categories of meditation into which all the meditations of the world can be fitted...The first category is breath or breathing meditations, second is point or area (cakra in Sanskrit—cakka, in Pali), third is visualization, fourth is sound, fifth is movement or mudra, sixth is devotional (emotional), seventh is essence of mind or insight. From Body Speech and Mind, A manual for human development, based on lectures by Namgyal RInpoche as heard by Cecilie Kwiat, (Bodhi Publishing, Kinmount Ontario Canada, 2004,) p.39
   man= mind tra= tools therefore mantra means a "mind tool" as heard by Charlene Jones in lecture with Namgyal Rinpoche

7. Samatha: calm, quietude of heart, calm and intuition, also means "for promoting calm" Pali Text Society, Pali-

English Dictionary

8. Sunyata: Sunnata: void, empty, devoid of lusts or evil dispositions and karma but especially of soul, ego

9. Tantra: "Tantra means thread, string, and implies connection. " Pali Text Society Pali-English Dictionary

10. Vajrayana: "The Vajrayana teaching is meant to accomplish totality of movement, to co-ordinate (body, speech and mind) so that they move together. When this occurs, it is equivalent to transcendental attainment." Body, Speech and Mind, A manual for Human Development as heard by Cecilie Kwiat,

11. Vipassana: inward, vision, insight, intuition, introspection: see Samatha by contrast

12. Visudhimagga: one of two oldest texts on meditation. The Visudhimagga describes 40 meditation practices. The other text is called the Vimmuthimagga and contains 38 meditation exercises

13. Wong or Wongkur: the name of the Empowerment ceremony, also called the Initiation Ceremony that forms the centre of Tibetan Buddhist Vajrayana Tantra practice

Bibliography

2. His Holiness Sakya Trizen heads the sect of Tibetan Buddhism called Sakya. For more on the other sects and their heads see Endnotes.

2. For more on Wongs or Empowerments go to www.khandro.net click on site map and scroll down on the left hand side to Tibetan Buddhism. Click and again scroll down on the left hand side to find the word Empowerment. Click on that for a clear, simple but full explanation of the role these ceremonies play in Vajrayana Tantra.

2. Mount Laurel Karmapa Visit…During First Dharma Center Visit, Karmapa teaches on…(April 4, 2015 Mount Laurel New Jersey)

2. Rita Carter, Mapping the Mind, (London, England The Orion Group, 1988), 14

2. Norman Doidge, <u>The Brain That Changes Itself, (New York,</u> Penguin Group, 2007), 48

2. Stephen Larsen, Ph.D., <u>The Neurofeedback Solution,</u> (Vermont, Healing Arts Press, 2012), 28

1. Doidge, op. cit., p. 48.

1. Ibid., p. 49.

1. Ibid, p. 187.

1. Doidge op. cit., p.189-190.

1. Doidge, op. cit., p. 194.

1. M. Iacoboni, <u>Mirroring People,</u>)New York, New York Farrar, Straus and Giroux, 2008) p.4

1. Ibid. p.11

1. Ibid. p.12

15. Ibid. p. 5

1. Ibid. p.5

1. Doidge, op. cit., p.214

1. N. Doidge, <u>The Brain's Way of Healing,</u> (New York, New York, Penguin Group, 2014) p.12

1. Ibid, p. 11

1. Ibid, p. 11-12

1. Ibid., p.15.

1. Ibid., p. 16

1. Ibid., p.16.

1. Ibid, p. 16

1. Ibid, p. 17

1. Ibid, p. 17

1. Ibid, p. 17

1. Ibid, p. 18

1. Bjorn van der Hoort, Arvid Guterstam, H. Henrik
    Ehrsson, May 25, 2011,
    DOI:10:1371/journal/pone/0020195 PLOS one.

1. Valeria Petkova, H. Henrik Ehrsson, "If I Were You:
    Perceptual Illusion of Body Swapping" December 3,
    2008, DOI:10:13711/Journal.pone.0003832

31. N.Doidge, The Brain's Way of Healing, (New York,
New York, Penguin Group, 2014) Contents

Endnotes

From www.aboutreligion.com by Barbara O'Brien

Buddhism first reached Tibet in the 7th century. By the 8th century teachers such as Padmasambhava were traveling to Tibet to teach the dharma. In time Tibetans developed their own perspectives and approaches to the Buddhist path. The list below is of the major distinctive traditions of Tibetan Buddhism. This is only a brief glimpse of traditions that have branched into many sub-schools and lineages.

1. Nyingma

Nyingma is the oldest school of Tibetan Buddhism. It claims as its founder Padmasambhava, also called Guru Rinpoche, "Beloved Master," which places its beginning in the late 8th century. Padmasambhava is credited with building Samye, the first monastery in Tibet, in about 779 CE.

Along with tantric practices, Nyingma emphasizes revealed teachings attributed to Padmasambhava plus the "great perfection" or Dzogchen doctrines. More »

2. Kagyu

The Kagyu school emerged from the teachings of Marpa "The Translator" (1012-1099) and his student, Milarepa. Milarepa's student Gampopa is the main founder of Kagyu. Kagyu is best known for its system of meditation and practice called Mahamudra.

The head of the Kagyu school is called the Karmapa. The current head is the Seventeenth Gyalwa Karmapa, Ogyen Trinley Dorje, who was born in 1985 in the Lhathok region of Tibet. More »

3. Sakya

In 1073, Khon Konchok Gyelpo (1034-1102) built Sakya Monastery in southern Tibet. His son and successor, Sakya Kunga Nyingpo, founded the Sakya sect. Sakya teachers converted the Mongol leaders Godan Khan and Kublai Khan to Buddhism. Over time, the Sakya school expanded to two subsects called the Ngor lineage and the Tsar lineage. Sakya, Ngor and Tsar constitute the three schools (*Sa-Ngor-Tsar-gsum*) of the Sakya tradition. The central teaching and practice of the Sakyapa is called *Lamdrey* (Lam-'bras), or "the Path and Its Fruit." The headquarters of the Sakya sect today are at Rajpur in Uttar Pradesh, India. The current head is the Sakya Trizin,

Ngakwang Kunga Thekchen Palbar Samphel Ganggi Gyalpo. More »

4. Gelug

The Gelug school, sometimes called the "yellow hat" sect of Tibetan Buddhism, was founded by Je Tsongkhapa (1357-1419), one of Tibet's greatest scholars. The first Gelug monastery, Ganden, was built by Tsongkhapa in 1409.

The Dalai Lamas, who have been spiritual leaders of the Tibetan people since the 17th century, come from the Gelug school. The nominal head of Gelugpa is the Ganden Tripa, an appointed official. The current Ganden Tripa is Thubten Nyima Lungtok Tenzin Norbu.

The Gelug school places great emphasis on monastic discipline and sound scholarship.More »

5. Jonang

Jonang was founded in the late 13th century by a monk named Kunpang Tukje Tsondru. Jonang is distinguished chiefly by kalachakra, its approach to tantra yoga.

In the 17th century the 5th Dalai Lama forcibly converted the Jonangs into his school, Gelug. Jonang was thought to be extinct as an independent school. However, in time it was learned that a few Jonang monasteries had maintained independence from Gelug.

Jonang is now officially recognized as an independent tradition once again. More »

6. Bonpo

When Buddhism arrived in Tibet it competed with indigenous traditions for the loyalty of Tibetans. These indigenous tradition combined elements of animism and shamanism. Some of the shaman priests of Tibet were called "bon," and in time "Bon" became the name of the non-Buddhist religious traditions that lingered in Tibetan culture.

In time elements of Bon were absorbed into Buddhism. At the same time, Bon traditions absorbed elements of Buddhism, until Bonpo seemed more Buddhist than not. Adherents of Bon consider their tradition to be separate from Buddhism. However, His Holiness the 14th Dalai Lama has recognized Bonpo as a school of Tibetan Buddhism.

If you enjoyed this book, please let your friends know about it!

Get Charlene Jones' novel on Reincarnationa called The Stain offered on her   website at www.soulsciences.net

stream her radio broadcasts from www.whistleradio.com 102.7 fm

Tune into her podcasts on iTunes called Soulsciences

contact Charlene at charlenej@rogers.com She loves hearing from readers!

Printed in Great
Britain
by Amazon